● Fun with El

Wittering & Waffling

How to say what you mean

Norman Barrett
Illustrated by Peter Stevenson

WOOF!

Chambers

Editor: John Grisewood

Illustrations: Peter Stevenson
(Kathy Jakeman Illustration)

CHAMBERS
An imprint of Larousse plc
Elsley House, 24-30 Great Titchfield Street,
London W1P 7AD

First published by Chambers 1995

2 4 6 8 10 9 7 5 3 1

Illustrations copyright © Larousse plc 1995
Text © Norman Barrett 1995

A CIP catalogue record for this book is available
from the British Library.

ISBN 0 550 32509 3

Printed in Spain

Contents

1 Worn-out words

How can words get worn out? The simple answer is overuse. Just as a person can become stale from overwork, so can words.

How often do you hear people repeating words or phrases such as 'basically' or 'sort of' every sentence or two while they are talking? The words seem to have lost any meaning, and are used merely as 'fillers' or 'crutches' on which to rest other, more important, words and ideas. Phrases used or made up by writers or broadcasters often become popular, and are then misused by people. Such phrases are called 'clichés' (see page 31). 'Avoid clichés like the plague' is good advice even though it is itself a hackneyed expression.

Er, obviously it's sort of basically no way, actually.

One cliché that has been around for at least 400 years is 'when all is said and done', meaning 'all things considered' or simply 'nevertheless'. A more modern version is 'at the end of the day'. A successful football coach once said, when his team were criticized for dull play: 'At the end of the day, I'll wake up in the morning, and the Cup will be in our trophy cabinet.'

Crutches

While it may be difficult to speak and write without using clichés at all, 'crutches' should perhaps be avoided. The simplest of these aids to speaking are 'um' and 'er'. When asked a question that makes you pause for thought, you might find one of these wretched little creatures useful, if

only to let the questioner know you are giving the matter your attention. But don't make a habit of it.

There is a whole group of 'crutch' words like 'basically', which we could dispense with altogether. They include 'actually', 'essentially', 'fundamentally', 'really', 'obviously' and phrases such as 'of course', 'in my view', 'the point is', 'in fact', 'the fact is', 'the fact of the matter is', and 'it's obvious to me'. We all use them from time to time.

Other irritating little expressions include: 'No way', 'I kid you not', 'I tell a lie', 'I like it' (after a joke), 'Know what I mean?' and ' I must love you and leave you'.

All these clichés are really, as a matter of fact, all things being equal, fairly harmless. But using a cliché suggests that a person cannot take the trouble to express his or her thoughts in a clear, fresh and imaginative way. Isn't it better to express your own thoughts in your own way? What do you think?

Ask a silly question

Sports stars are among the biggest culprits when it comes to the use of clichés. Some are not very articulate, unlike, say, politicians or lawyers whose professions depend on being able to speak coherently.

Perhaps the fault lies more with the interviewers who ask some silly, unimaginative questions. When a boxer, who has just been knocked out and is lying sprawled across the canvas, arms dangling down over the ringside and chin sagging on the rope, has a microphone thrust under his battered and bleeding nose and is asked, 'How do you feel about losing your title, Rocky?', it is not surprising when he delivers the classic response, 'Sick as a parrot, Barry'.

I'm over the moon ... sick as a parrot

The winner's cliché in such circumstances is 'Over the moon!' But can we really expect a footballer, say, as he comes off the field, hot sweating and exhausted, to give an original or eloquent answer to some enquiries about his feelings. What would you say if asked how you felt after winning something, a school prize, perhaps, or a sporting trophy?

See how many 'Over the moon' clichés you can think up — there are some in the answers (page 27).

'Most of my clichés aren't original'

A veteran American football coach recently came out with a gem of a quote. 'Most of my clichés aren't original,' he said. Of course, a cliché would not be a cliché if it were an original phrase or saying. Every cliché was original once. Many were very clever or fitting. That's why they caught on. And used in the right place, clichés can still be effective. You just have to be careful, as an American Vice-President found out when he said: 'There's a lot of uncharted waters in space.'

When there's been some interference in a TV or radio programme, say, it is customary for an announcer to apologize with a phrase like 'We hope it did not spoil your enjoyment of ...' This is a perfectly reasonable thing to say, but, again, when you are using a stock phrase, give a little thought as to whether it is appropriate. The radio presenter who made the following announcement obviously didn't: 'We would like to welcome back listeners and apologize for the 20-minute break in transmission. We hope it didn't spoil your enjoyment of Thirty-Minute Theatre.'

The uncharted waters of space

Clichés come in all shapes and sizes (to use another cliché!). Here are some more, ancient and modern, with one of the words missing. Perhaps you know some of them or can guess the missing word. Their meanings are given to help you (answers on page 27):

1 The time is ... (The moment has come for action or for something to happen)
2 A ... diamond (A person with crude manners but who shows great promise)
3 Grit your ... (Prepare for a difficult experience)
4 A ... from the blue (A complete shock)
5 Every ... has a silver lining (There is hope in any situation)
6 Stick-in-the- ... (A dull person who does not like change or what others regard as progress)
7 On the ... of the moment (On an impulse, without thinking first)
8 Shot in the ... (A wild guess)
9 Tighten your ... (Prepare to economize)
10 My ... half (My wife, or husband)
11 ... playing field (Starting on even terms)
12 ... the goal-posts (Changing the rules without telling the people involved)
13 Give the ... light to (Give permission to go ahead)
14 Beat about the ... (Talk about a subject without coming to the point)
15 Take the bull by the ...(Face a difficulty boldly)
16 Talk though your ... (Talk nonsense)
17 To sell like hot ... (Be a success)
18 Turn over a new ... (Start again)
19 City of ... Spires (Oxford)
20 The ... Isle (Ireland)

Waist not, want not

7

2 It's another language

All languages have idioms. An idiom is an expression, usually a group of two or more words, that has a special meaning, different from what the meaning would be if you took the words separately. 'Red tape', for example, means official procedures that slow people down when they are trying to get something done. Neither of the words, 'red' or 'tape', has anything to do with the meaning of the expression. And if you tried to translate it into a foreign language, it would not help to look up these words separately in a dictionary.

When computer programmes were first designed for translating words into foreign languages, idioms caused plenty of trouble. The proverb 'Out of sight, out of mind' (which means you are likely to be forgotten or over-looked unless you make yourself noticed) was fed into a computer to translate it into Russian, and out came two Russian words meaning 'blind idiot'. You can understand the work-ing of the computer. 'Blind' means having lost one's sight ('out of' meaning 'none left', as in 'we're out of bread'), and an 'idiot' is out of his or her mind.

It was not a Russian computer, however, that wrote a sign in English at Moscow airport saying: IF THIS IS YOUR FIRST VISIT TO RUSSIA YOU ARE WELCOME TO IT.
Do you see what's wrong with this? If not, the answer is on page 27.

To 'have a child' means to give birth, but the person who wrote this sign in a Norwegian hotel did not seem to know this: LADIES ARE REQUESTED NOT TO HAVE CHILDREN IN THE BAR.

You all come back now!

You can be confused by idioms in your own language. But if you have not come across a particular phrase before, you can sometimes work out what it means from the way it is used. If you heard, for example, that a class 'fell about' when their teacher sat on his hat, you can picture them helpless with laughter — you don't think that they 'fell' anywhere.

But it is almost impossible to work out that the idiom 'fly a kite' means 'to test public opinion, or to spread a rumour'.

All the different dialects of English have their own idioms and special expressions. The English spoken in Scotland, say, or in the American South, not only sounds very different from Standard English (see page 31), but uses many special words and phrases with entirely different meanings.

There are countless stories of English people in America or Americans in England completely misunderstanding the local language. Typical is the one about the Englishman somewhere in the southern United States who was just about to leave a supermarket when he heard someone call out: 'Y'arl [You all] come back now', and, thinking he had left something behind, he went back! He did not realize that this was just a friendly southern way of saying, 'We hope to see you again'.

There is no clear distinction between a useful idiom or phrase and a cliché. Not all idioms are clichés. Take these idioms for example:

much of a muchness (not very different)

to pull your punches (to use less force in attacking than one is capable of)

to have the best of both worlds (to benefit from the best of two different sets of circumstances)

rise to the occasion (to be able to do what is required in an emergency)

The best advice is to use idioms — and clichés — sparingly.

Falling about ...

See if you can complete the following expressions or idioms with the help of the clues in brackets (answers page 28):

1 Fair ... friend (A friend who deserts you when you are in trouble)
2 ... out of water (Someone in unfamiliar company or surroundings)
3 Keep the ... boiling (Keep something going or on the move)
4 The bee's ... (The best at something)

The bee's ...

5 Bursting at the ... (Over-full, packed tight)
6 ... refusal (An option to buy something before it is offered to anyone else)
7 To see ... (To become angry)
8 Make a ... out of a molehill (To exaggerate a problem, make much out of little)
9 Turn a ... eye to (Allow misbehaviour to pass, pretending not to notice)
10 Run of the ... (Average)
11 A wild goose ... (A search doomed to be unsuccessful)
12 A ... of contention (Something which causes disagreement)
13 Make no ... about it (Admit without fuss or bother)
14 A blessing in ... (Something which proves to be fortunate after appearing to be unfortunate)

A different kettle of fish

Expressions come about for all kinds of reasons. 'Red tape' comes from the old custom of government officials tying up their papers with red ribbons. The origin of some expressions is fairly obvious. 'Off the record', for example, means unofficial' — not written in the records.

Some expressions become so regularly misused that they take on a new meaning. Take, for instance, 'a different kettle of fish'. In the sentence, 'She is very good at charades, but taking part in the school play will be a different kettle of fish,' the phrase means more difficult or demanding. The 'kettle' in this

15 Bored to ... (Bored beyond endurance)

16 A ... in one's ear (A sharp scolding)

17 Stick one's ... in (Interfere with what somebody else is doing)

18 Prick up one's ... (Start to pay attention)

19 By the ... of one's teeth (Very narrowly)

20 Be in the ... (Be involved)

21 Take ... leave (To be absent without permission)

22 Add ... to the fire (Make an angry person angrier)

23 Pull one's ... up (Make an effort to do better)

24 Go like a ... (Go very fast)

25 Waste one's ... (Say something that is not listened to)

A wild goose ...

expression comes from an old word 'kiddle', which was a kind of basket set in a stream to catch fish. A 'kettle of fish' came to be used for the picnic of freshly caught salmon. Then it was used to mean an upheaval or mess (often with the word 'pretty'), as in 'Well, that's a pretty kettle of fish: all the children have arrived for the party, the entertainer's caught in traffic, the sandwiches haven't defrosted and the dog's been sick on the carpet after eating the birthday cake.'

What, one wonders, would the Russian translation computer have made of 'kettle of fish'? Probably 'boiled sturgeon'!

3 Mixed blessings

The English language is rich in expressions which we use for conveying different meanings. People enjoy using expressions to get an idea across or to emphasize a point. If you overuse them, they become clichés. But there is another trap for the unwary — mixing them up. This usually comes from trying to be too clever, as in: 'That snake in the grass is barking up the wrong tree.'

'A snake in the grass' means a hidden enemy, someone you might consider as a friend but who betrays you. And someone 'barking up the wrong tree' has got the wrong idea or is accusing the wrong person. But when you put the two expressions together, you've got a 'barking snake'.

Here's a beauty from a union leader, with three expressions that don't really go together: 'The company stabbed us in the back by blowing the talks out of the water before they even got off the ground.'

If someone confused burning the midnight oil (meaning working or studying very late — people once used oil lamps for light) with burning the candle at both ends (working very hard and doing so many other things that you are exhausted) they could get 'burn the midnight oil at both ends'!

A snake in the grass barking up the wrong tree

WOOF!

Which two expressions have been confused in each of the following? (answers on page 28)

1 It's as easy as falling off a piece of cake.
2 He'll just have to swallow the bullet.
3 She took the bull by the tail.
4 He was out of his rocker.
5 Are we going to sit back and take this lying down?
6 He is leading the people over a precipice with his head in the sand.
7 I smell a rat, but we shall nip it in the bud.
8 You can't teach an old dog to suck eggs.

4 A lot of waffle

It's called 'gobbledygook' — all that waffle you meet in rules and regulations, forms to be filled in, instructions for working machines, and even on medicine labels. Among the worst culprits are solicitors. They fill their documents with jargon that the ordinary person finds impossible to understand. And they are never content to use one word when three or four will do.

In a typical sales contract you will find a lot of waffle in the conditions printed in small type on the back. Small type has to be used to cram all the words in. Take, for example, the condition occurring if a buyer fails to complete payment. Instead of starting 'if the buyer defaults', it would say, 'in the event of default on the part of the buyer ...' — eleven words instead of four.

A fine example of waffle — from a conference of sociologists in America in 1977 — is recorded by Bill Bryson in his book *Mother Tongue*. See if you can work out what the author of these words is trying to define (answer on page 28): 'The cognitive-affective state characterized by intrusive and obsessive fantasizing concerning reciprocity of amorant feelings by the object of the amorance.'

The habit is catching

The language used in legal documents is often referred to as 'legalese' — a language that only lawyers themselves can understand. Unfortunately, the habit is catching. People drawing up rules of any kind feel they have to write them in the dreaded legalese.

Take the game of football. The law-makers of football have always insisted that it is a simple game. Yet the following — just one example — found its way into the rule book. Note particularly the last bit, in **bold** type.

'If a player taking a goal-kick plays the ball a second time after it has passed beyond the penalty area, but before it has touched or been played by another player, an indirect free-kick shall be awarded to the opposing team, to be taken from the place where the infringement occurred, **unless the offence is committed by a player in his opponents' goal-area, in which case, the free-kick shall be taken from a point anywhere within that half of the goal-area in which the offence occurred.'**

The 51 words of the first part appear to be quite straightforward. But the 35 words of the second part are completely unnecessary. They refer to an event that cannot reasonably be expected to happen. It certainly has never happened in football as played

Playing by the rules ...

on this planet, at least not outside the game of table soccer.

If you understand just a little about football, and you have the patience to read the piece again, you will see that the offending player has to take the goal-kick and then run some 100 metres to the opposite goal area and play the ball again before anyone else does! (Those 35 words stayed in the laws of the game for several years before intelligence came to the rescue and they were finally replaced.)

A bed is a bed — or is it?

The word 'bed' has a few meanings. In the house it's what you sleep on and in the garden it's what you plant flowers in. There are sea beds, river-beds and oyster-beds. You might find your food in a restaurant served on a bed of rice or a bed of lettuce. And so on. Narrowing it

down to the bed you sleep on, there are single beds, double beds, sofa-beds, four-poster beds and so on. There are also hospital beds. In some places these might be expensive pieces of machinery that can be controlled electrically to move up and down, tilt, provide vibrations and do just about everything but bath the patient.

But whatever kind of hospital bed you are talking about, you would not expect to use 163 words to define it. Yet that is how many words were needed by a health authority in Wales. The endless definition started off like this:

Bed A device or arrangement that may be used to permit a patient to lie down when the need to do so is a consequence of the patient's condition rather than a need for active intervention such as examination, diagnostic investigation, manipulative treatment, obstetric delivery or transport. Beds, couches, or trolleys are also counted as hospital beds where: a) used regularly to permit a patient to lie down rather than for merely examination or transport ....

That's 75 words — not even half the definition! No doubt, the authority had its reasons for wanting to know exactly how many 'beds' there were in each hospital under its control — but this is a real 'daffy-nition'!

Concise gobbledygook

That sample of gobbledygook won an 'award' from the Plain English Campaign, an organization set up to protect the public from jargon and other nonsense. It is certainly not the worst example they have unearthed. And something does not have to be long-winded to be classified as gobbledygook. A sports commentator describing an international netball match told viewers that one of the players 'gets good vertical elevation' — meaning, presumably, that she jumps high. He must have swallowed a coaching handbook.

Costly gobbledygook

Most gobbledygook is wasteful. The time spent by people wading through lots of meaningless jargon must cost millions of pounds every year. And the confusion caused can be expensive, too. In 1992, a British hotel

chain spent over £300,000 on unnecessary inspection of electrical equipment just because a mistake was made in interpreting regulations. According to the Plain English Campaign, sloppy letter-writing costs Britain about £6 billion a year as the result of mistakes, inefficiency and lost business.

Jargon — good and bad

The word jargon is used in two senses. The first sense, according to *The Chambers Dictionary*, is 'the specialized vocabulary of a particular trade, profession, group, or activity'. So there is computer jargon (with its bytes and interfaces), banking jargon

GOBBLEDYGOOK

Here are some short examples of gobbledygook. See if you can interpret them (answers on page 29):

1 These spreads run quite close together on the pagination.
   (Publishing memo)
2 Was your Uniform Business Rate demand subject to transitional phasing arrangements?
3 I must convey to you my goodwill in a correspondence format.
   (Apology for absence)
4 We do not contemplate the possibility that such a thing will eventuate.
5 They partook of the first meal of the day.

WAS YOUR UNIFORM BUSINESS RATE DEMAND SUBJECT TO TRANSITIONAL PHASING ARRANGEMENTS?

(with its foreclosings and letters of credit), printing jargon (with its ems, points and medium bold sans serifs). At its best, jargon is useful as a kind of professional shorthand used by experts.

The second — derogatory — definition of jargon is 'confusing or meaningless talk'. In this sense it goes back to its French root — 'meaningless chatter, gibberish'.

When jargon strays from being the useful technical shorthand of a trade or profession and is used to impress, mystify or browbeat those outside the 'magic circle', it then becomes 'meaningless chatter'.

Jargon is closely related to 'gobbledygook', which itself can be defined as incomprehensible language because of the use of too many long words — verbiage. Verbiage often sounds impressive and may use 'vogue words' and euphemisms (*economy-size* for small, *evergreens* for old people). Too often language can be used not to convey ideas clearly but merely to sound impressive. You have been warned!

5 Same again

'The place from whence Grock came was very unique, and he would often recall back his past history, when fellow class-mates were few in number, and Mr Sweeney, just before he ascended upwards to heaven, assembled them together and prophesied that they had a great future ahead of them.'

This is the opening sentence of a short story that has not yet been written. And if the author carries on like this, it will end up a long one, because everything is said twice. 'Whence' means from where, so 'from whence' is like saying 'from from where'. Nothing can be 'very unique' — 'unique' means the only one, so either it's unique or it's not. In the same way, 'recall' is to bring back to mind, 'history' can only be past, 'fellow' implies mates and 'few' implies number. The only direction in which you 'ascend' is upwards, 'assemble' means to bring together, and your 'future' can only be ahead of you.

The unnecessary use of words in this way to say the same thing is called 'tautology'. Words used needlessly are 'redundant'. See if you can rewrite the opening sentence at the top of the page without using redundant words. (answer on page 29)

I CAN'T STAND ANY MORE TAUTOLOGY

See if you can find the redundant words in the following and say why (answers on page 29):

1 It was their habitual custom to eat out on Mondays.
2 The boat's speed was 20 knots per hour.
3 His eyes protrude out of their sockets.
4 Her words were like a pointed barb to his heart.
5 Santa distributed free gifts to all the young people.
6 There was no other alternative but to resign.
7 Sally has drawn a four-sided square on the board.
8 At that time the motor car was a new innovation.
9 This is the most wettest weather we've had for years.
10 It's even more worse than last year.

TAUTOLOGY

Together, back and again are commonly misused with words that do not need them, as in 'revive again'. 'Revive' means to bring back to life as in 'she revived the half-drowned child', or to return to a fresh lively state, as in 'flowers revive in water', or it can mean to return to use, as in 'revive an old play'. The Latin root of the word — *revivere* — means to live again.

Well housed

Can you find the tautology in this piece from a newspaper? 'Ex-Beatle George Harrison has created a fantasy world at his home in Henley. Beneath the house are a series of caverns, half-filled with water, where illuminated gnomes peep from the rocks, and the 34-acre gardens contain a huge fountain, a waterfall, and a scaled-down model of the Matterhorn (a famous Swiss mountain).'
(answer on page 29)

They're back together again ...
All of the following words should usually stand alone, but are often misused with either 'together', 'back' or 'again'. Do you know the meaning of these words? (answers on page 29) Clue — all the answers should contain either 'together', 'back' or 'again', except one, which has 'of'.

1 congregate
2 recoil
3 fuse
4 merge
5 renew
6 recur
7 retreat
8 repeat
9 comprise
10 restart
11 retract
12 interlink

SALLY HAS DRAWN A FOUR SIDED SQUARE

6 That is an ex-parrot

People often find the need to use a pleasant or mild word for an idea they find offensive or distressing. They talk about a person having 'passed away' instead of having died. Or they might use 'tummy' for 'belly' or 'stout' instead of 'fat'.

The word for such expressions is 'euphemism', from a Greek word meaning 'to speak favourably'. All kinds of people use it. In politics, for instance, a 'lie' becomes an 'inoperative statement'. In war, a million deaths becomes a 'megadeath'.

Dealing with death

People have always found it difficult to talk about death, and have invented countless phrases to avoid mentioning the dreaded word, from the genteel 'she has gone to a better place' to the crude 'he's croaked'.

Here are some more variations,of both kinds, for death or died: 'breathed his last', 'snuffed it', 'bowed out', 'passed over', 'the final curtain', 'popped off', 'kicked the bucket', 'cashed in his chips', 'the final summons', 'went west', 'joined the immortals', 'called it quits', 'went the way of all flesh', 'checked out', 'gone to the last round-up'.

And the person or firm that has to deal with the bodies (remains) of the dead — the undertaker — is a euphemism for 'undertaker of burials'. This euphemism has itself been replaced by 'funeral director' and the American 'mortician'.

In the 'dead parrot' sketch from *Monty Python's Flying Circus*, the customer trying to convince the pet-shop owner that the bird he had bought was dead uses all kinds of euphemisms to get his point across, finishing up with 'This is an ex-parrot!'.

All frogs must croak in the end.

EUPHEMISMS

It is understandable that people in the business of killing will try to dress up their occupation with fancy words. Gangsters spoke of having their victims 'bumped off', 'removed', 'liquidated' or 'taken for a ride'. In modern military terms, killing the enemy might be called 'servicing the target', and the accidental killing of civilians referred to as 'collateral damage'.

> The most notorious euphemism for killing was 'the final solution' *(die Endlösung)*, a term used by the Nazis to cover up the mass extermination of Jews in the 1930s and 1940s.

Probably the most ridiculous term for death was invented for use in American hospitals — 'negative patient care outcome'.

The unmentionables

Perhaps the biggest collection of euphemisms has grown up for 'unmentionable' parts of the body and for natural 'bodily functions'. No sooner does one word or phrase become 'vulgar' than another is coined. So we have euphemisms for euphemisms! All kinds of names have been devised to avoid using the term 'lavatory' — privy, ladies' or gents' (room), WC (water closet), little boys' (girls') room, powder room, rest room, bathroom, the smallest room, comfort station, wash-room, urinal, convenience, facilities — yet 'lavatory' itself is a euphemism, coming from the Latin word *lavatorium*, meaning 'a place for washing'. Among the most popular modern names are 'loo' (British — probably from the French word *l'eau*, meaning water), 'the john' (US) and 'dunny' (Australian).

Going to the loo can be 'spending a penny', 'answering the call of nature' or 'seeing a man about a dog'. Asking permission to go can be, 'May I please be excused?'

Harmless and kind

Most of these euphemisms are quite harmless, and if you know people will be offended by blunt words, it is silly to use them. In any case, you can avoid the more ludicrous euphemisms.

Sometimes it is kinder to use a euphemism. Many people would probably prefer to be asked to look for alternative employment than to be told bluntly that they are dismissed, sacked or fired. But to call the hard-of-hearing and the deaf 'hearing impaired' only glosses over their disability. It is usually preferable to use plain, everyday language, so there is no reason why anyone should not 'sweat' after exercise, although some may prefer to 'perspire'; and talk about 'rich' or 'poor' people rather than 'wealthy' or 'disadvantaged' people.

It is quite a different matter when people use euphemisms to hide the truth for their own advantage or avoid giving an honest answer.

Here are some euphemisms that have been or might be used in various activities. See if you can work out what they are 'hiding' (answers on page 30):

1 Activities incompatible with diplomatic status (Excuse for expelling member of embassy staff)
2 He did not fully achieve his wellness potential (Hospital bulletin)
3 Correctional facility
4 Terminological inexactitude
5 Economical with the truth
6 He'll be disappointed with that shot (Sports commentator)
7 The lower income brackets
8 Achieving schedule overrun
9 For your added comfort and convenience (Advice on hotel-room door to lock it)
10 Her contract has been terminated
11 People waiting for jobs
12 Full figured

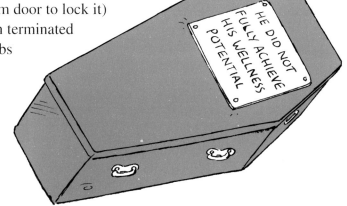

7 Persongling the language

Language is always changing. New words are added and old ones die out. There is no official list of English words, but the new single-volume Chambers Dictionary, *for example, has 300,000 definitions.*

Many dictionaries publish supplements every so often listing new words and meanings. These might include colloquialisms (words used in familiar talk) such as 'gobsmacked' and 'high-five', 'glass ceiling' and 'retrolutionary'. They might also include words such as 'street cred', 'zapper', 'personkind' and 'waitperson'.

Many such awkward-sounding words with 'person' have been introduced to the language largely to avoid 'sexist' expressions. It is true that the language is 'sexist' — biased towards the male. Words such as 'spokesman' and 'chairman' seem to stress male importance, whereas they should, of course, include women. 'Mankind', which means all people, and the word 'man' itself are being replaced by expressions such as humankind and human beings. But there are also what many regard as ugly, ridiculous inventions such as 'personkind'.

Ms in the chair

In recent years the title 'Ms' for Miss or Mrs has been introduced and generally accepted. The idea was to find a title for women that matches the neutral Mr for men and tells us nothing about the woman's status — whether she is married or not. The replacement of 'chairman' by 'chair' is also now well established and cleverly avoids the ambiguous appeal to 'Madam Chair**man**!' It is also a much better word than the cumbersome 'chairperson'. And for centuries they have had in the House of Commons a 'speaker' who until a few years ago always happened to be Mr Speaker. In 1992 the office was filled by a Madam Speaker.

Madam chair

Waitperson please

both sexes) can be found — for example 'firefighter' seems very acceptable, and in reverse 'nurse' can now be male or female.

Problem pronouns

Here's an extract from a book about karting: 'The driver sits very close to the ground. He wears a safety helmet ...' But why should the driver be a boy? Surely girls also enjoy karting.

This is a problem. The only way to solve it in English without being sexist is to write: 'He or she wears a helmet.' That's all right once or twice, but when it's repeated again and again it becomes tiresome.

What the language needs are pronouns that mean 'he or she', 'his or her' and 'him or her'. Again, any ideas? How about 'hes' for 'his or her' and 'hem' for 'him or her'? You would say: 'The driver must always wear hes [his or her] helmet.'

If a man and a woman do a job equally well, why call them by different names? For example, why waiters and waitresses? There is no good reason. It has been suggested that a word like 'waitperson' with its plural either 'waitpersons' or 'waitpeople' would be a suitable replacement. But they are pretty ugly monsters of words, don't you agree? How about 'server' as an alternative? Any other suggestions?

And isn't it rather unimaginative, every time 'man' is used in a word that refers to both sexes to replace it with 'person'. More acceptable 'inclusive' words (words that include

Neutral and non-sexist

supervisor *for* foreman
astronaut *for* spaceman
staffed by *for* manned by
bartender *for* bar maid
poet *for* poetess
author *for* authoress
sculptor *for* sculptress
flight attendant *for* stewardess

The mad computerperson

Imagine a crazy computer program for neutralizing sexist words. Try putting the following paragraph back to what it was before it had been 'persongled' (see answers page 30):

The newsperson, looking at the peopleu, complained about the price of the ploughperson's lunch to the barperson, who called Theirperson, the Gerperson doorperson. That neutervolent personiac personhandled the pressperson out of the chickentail lounge, over the pavepersonst, into a pile of personure and down an open personhole. This turned out to be a faux parents, for the newspaperperson changed into Superperson and returned to the oxy to disswanse punishpersonst.

8 PC mania

It is a good thing to want to rid the language of words or expressions whose very use cause offence to some people. There are many terms, used innocently (or otherwise) for years, which may be hurtful to the people they are used to describe - such as fat, crippled, deaf, short, bald, ugly, stupid, old. But to call someone who is bald 'hair disadvantaged' may only draw more attention to it. And it is an ugly nonsensical expression. What do you think?

To be 'politically correct' (PC), does not really have anything to do with politics. It is a way of dressing up terms that might give offence in language that is supposed not to give offence. Unfortunately, it often does not work. Many of the well-meaning but silly euphemisms (see page 19) are monstrously ugly and impossible to use in conversation.

Imagine describing someone as 'differently sized', which is one PC term for 'fat': 'Which one of the boys in the picture is Fred?' 'Oh, he's the differently sized one at the front.' What about a film review starting like this? 'The vertically challenged, differently sized, hair disadvantaged, cosmetically different Danny DeVito was perfect in the part of Owen Lift, a short, fat, bald, ugly, would-be mystery writer who ....'

This is an exaggeration, of course, but the trouble with political correctness is that much of it is so laughable, you can't tell the difference between the real thing and the inventions of those who make fun of it.

A person of substance wearing a size-friendly shirt

Although the intentions of those who practise political correctness are mostly honourable, you cannot force people to use words and phrases. You can only make suggestions. But if these are silly, you are probably wasting your time.

POLITICAL CORRECTNESS

To insist on calling white coffee 'coffee with milk' and black coffee 'coffee without milk' is rather silly. But to point out the fault in terms such as 'wheelchair-bound' and 'confined to a wheelchair' makes sense. Wheelchairs don't confine handicapped people. They help them to get around. So it is not only kinder, but more correct, to talk about 'wheelchair users'.

Which only goes to show that new ideas should be treated on their merits.

See if you can guess what the following PC terms, not all intended to be serious, are meant to replace (answers on page 30):

1 Meat dealer
2 Differently heighted
3 Aurally inconvenienced
4 Parentally disadvantaged
5 Rodent operative
6 Nonliving person
7 Charm-free
8 Herstory
9 Prewoman
10 Alternative dentation
11 Birth name
12 Efemcipation
13 Involuntarily leisured
14 Snow figure
15 Animal companion
16 Single-by-choice senior citizen
17 Intellectually challenged
18 Sewer access hole
19 Company representative
20 Chronologically challenged

ANSWERS

1 Worn-out words
Ask a silly question
(page 6)
Some 'Over the moon' clichés: delighted, absolutely delighted, highly pleased, well pleased, pleased as Punch, chuffed, elated, jubilant, ecstatic, overjoyed, proud, etc, etc.

Complete the clichés
(page 7)
1 *The time is ripe*
2 *A rough diamond*
3 *Grit your teeth*
4 *A bolt from the blue*

5 *Every cloud has a silver lining*
6 *Stick-in-the-mud*
7 *On the spur of the moment*
8 *Shot in the dark*
9 *Tighten your belt*
10 *My better half*
11 *Level playing field*

12 *Moving the goal-posts*
13 *Give the green light to*
14 *Beat about the bush*
15 *Take the bull by the horns*
16 *Talk through your hat*
17 *To sell like hot cakes*
18 *Turn over a new leaf*
19 *City of Dreaming Spires*
20 *The Emerald Isle*

2 It's another language
(page 8)
The writer of the sign knew the idiom 'welcome to it', but confused its meaning — a rude way of saying that someone deserves to get something unpleasant.

Complete the idioms
(page 10)

1 *Fair-weather friend*
2 *Fish out of water*
3 *Keep the pot boiling*
4 *The bee's knees*
5 *Bursting at the seams*
6 *First refusal*
7 *To see red*
8 *Make a mountain out of a molehill*
9 *Turn a blind eye to*
10 *Run of the mill*
11 *A wild goose chase*
12 *A bone of contention*
13 *Make no bones about it*
14 *A blessing in disguise*
15 *Bored to tears*
16 *A flea in one's ear*
17 *Stick one's oar in*
18 *Prick up one's ears*
19 *By the skin of one's teeth*
20 *Be in the swim (or thick)*
21 *Take French leave*
22 *Add fuel to the fire*
23 *Pull one's socks up*
24 *Go like a dream (or bomb)*
25 *Waste one's breath*

3 Mixed blessings
(page 12)

1 *Falling off a log and a piece of cake — both of which are said to be easy.*
2 *Swallow one's pride (to accept something even though you find it humiliating) and bite the bullet (to accept something unpleasant and face it with courage).*
3 *To take the bull by the horns (to tackle a difficult problem instead of avoiding it) and have a tiger by the tail (to hold on to an idea or obsession and refuse to let go).*
4 *Out of one's mind and off one's rocker both mean to be crazy or mad.*
5 *To sit back (take no part in) and to take something lying down (without complaining or arguing).*
6 *Over a precipice (to danger) and head in the sand (ignoring a problem).*
7 *Smell a rat (to suspect something is wrong) and nip it in the bud (to stop it as soon as it starts).*
8 *You can't teach an old dog new tricks (people set in their ways don't welcome change) and don't teach your grandmother to suck eggs (don't try to give advice to people more experienced than you).*

4 A lot of waffle
(page 13)

the 'cognitive-affective state...' is simply 'love'.

Gobbledygook (page 16):

1 'run quite close together on the pagination' — are close to each other

2 'transitional phasing arrangements' — (It was part of a question on a form, and I had to leave the answer blank because I didn't know what it meant. Can you have a guess?)

3 'convey to you my goodwill in a correspondence format' — 'wish you well by letter' (This was deliberate gobbledygook by HRH The Prince of Wales to the Plain English Campaign)

4 'We do not contemplate the possibility that such a thing will eventuate.' — We don't think it will happen.

5 'partook of the first meal of the day' — had breakfast.

5 Same again (page 17)

'The place whence Grock came was unique, and he would often recall his past, when classmates were few, and Mr Sweeney, just before he ascended to heaven, assembled them and prophesied that they had a great future.'

Redundant words (page 17)

1 habitual (a custom is habitual)

2 per hour (a knot is a nautical mile per hour)

3 out (say 'protrude from')

4 pointed (a barb is pointed)

5 free (gifts are free)

6 other (alternative is other)

7 four-sided (all squares have four sides)

8 new (innovations are new)

9 most (wettest is most wet)

10 more (worse is more bad)

Well housed (page 18)

'Scaled-down model' is the tautology. A model of the Matterhorn would have to be scaled down to fit into even the largest garden.

They're back together again (page 18)

1 congregate — come together in a crowd

2 recoil — spring or shrink back

3 fuse — mix together (by melting)

4 merge — join up or blend together

5 renew — make or begin again

6 recur — happen again

7 retreat — go back

8 repeat — say again

9 comprise — consist of

10 restart — start again

11 retract — take back

12 interlink — connect together

6 The ex-parrot (page 21) Euphemisms

1 *Activities incompatible with diplomatic status* — Spying
2 *He did not fully achieve his wellness potential* — He died
3 *Correctional facility* — Prison
4 *Terminological inexactitude* — A lie
5 *Economical with the truth* — Lying
6 *He'll be disappointed with that shot* — It was a poor shot
7 *The lower income brackets* — The poor
8 *Achieving schedule overrun* — Falling behind
9 *For your added comfort and convenience* — For your safety
10 *Her contract has been terminated* — She's been sacked
11 *People waiting for jobs* — The unemployed
12 *Full figured* — Fat

7 Persongling the language (page 24)

*The news**man**, looking at the **men**u, complained about the price of the plough**man**'s lunch to the bar**man**, who called **Herman**, the Ger**man** door**man**.*

*That **male**volent **man**iac **man**handled the press**man** out of the **cock**tail lounge, over the pave**men**t, into a pile of **man**ure and down an open **man**hole. This turned out to be a faux **pas**, for the newspaper**man** changed into Super**man** and returned to the **bull**y to dis**pen**se punish**men**t.*

8 PC mania (page 26)

1 *Butcher (this is an 'upgrading' of an occupation title, to avoid thoughts of killing animals)*
2 *Small*
3 *Deaf*
4 *An orphan*
5 *Rat-catcher (this term is 50 years old!)*
6 *Corpse*
7 *Dull and boring*
8 *History*
9 *Girl*

I'VE BEEN SACKED.

10 *False teeth*
11 *Maiden name*
12 *Emancipation — as it applies to the liberation of women*
13 *Unemployed*
14 *Snowman*

15 *Pet*
16 *Spinster*
17 *Stupid*
18 *Manhole*
19 *Spokesman*
20 *Old*

The word cliché comes from a French word meaning 'stereo-type'. A stereotype was originally a printing plate cast from a mould. The printing plate turns out the same page again and again. This gave rise to the idea of a phrase or idea being repeated again and again — to a trite, hackneyed expression, a cliché.

Standard English is the speech or 'dialect' of the upper and upper-middle classes. It is normally used in writing English and teaching it to foreigners.